THE MASTERPIECE PRICE

Book 6 Reflection of God Moments

56 One Minute Devotionals

Journal

The Masterpiece Price
Book 6 Reflections of God Moments
copyright © 2024

Written by: Donesa Walker
Design by: Will Baten
Edited by: Kelley Inderman

The Mountain of Praise!
Psalms 18:1-3, 6, 16-19, 30

What should you do when you're hurting/discouraged?

Why should we not stay on the mountaintop?

Key thought for today:

Unique and Adored!
Galatians 5:25-26

I am unique because....

Key thought for today:

Embracing Limitations!
2 Corinthians 12: 7-10

What do you feel are your limitations?

How can God help you to embrace this, so that you can walk in His Grace?

Key thought for today:

Jesus At The Center!
Psalms 19:7-10

Are you now, or have you ever lost your way and gotten off the path God set out for you? If so, how do you think you got there?

What are some ways that you can find your way back?

Key thought for today:

The Viewfinder!

Who or what is a source of irritation for you and why?

List any positive aspects or benefits of this irritation.

Key thought for today:

The Circumstances of Joy!
Luke 6:37-38

Have you encountered a situation or circumstance of life that has stolen your joy?

What are some things you can do to turn this negative into a positive?

Key thought for today:

Being Known As I Am!
Hebrews 10:19-25

You've been given an "audience" with the King; What will you do with this time?

How often do you fail to recognize the value of His forgiveness?

Key thought for today:

There's More To Come!
Romans 5:3-5

What one circumstance in your life is really trying your patience?

What can you do in anticipation of your "miracle"?

Key thought for today:

Parched But Growing!
John 14:1-4, 11-14

Do you trust God? If so, then are you yielding yourself to be used by the Master's Hand?

How are you allowing God to use/grow you right now?

Key thought for today:

Scattered By The Light!
John 3:19-21, 34-36

How do you keep your light shining?

Key thought for today:

What Came First?
John 1:1-5

What came first?

Do you think that the God Creator of all things doesn't know you?

Do you know Him? How can you know Him better?

Key thought for today:

The Contribution!
Isaiah 53:2-6

For whom was Jesus crucified and why?

What are you contributing to the "cause"?

Key thought for today:

Loving Loud!
John 13:34-35

What are some things that you can/are doing to Love Loud?

Key thought for today:

The Unseen Hand!
James 1:2-4

What do you think would happen if we truly embraced the storms of life as useful, understanding that He is forming us into the masterpiece of His design?

Key thought for today:

The Final Step In A Journey!
Romans 10:11-13

Do those around you know that He lives within you?

Key thought for today:

Reflecting Light!
Romans 3:3-4, 23-24

Are you a true reflection of His Sonlight? How does this look? What is your "happy" color?

Key thought for today:

The Why!
Matthew 28:16-20

What is the most important thing Jesus did after being raised from the dead? Why?

What does this mean for us today?

How do we go about doing this?

Key thought for today:

The Weighty Plan!
Isaiah 53:10-12

Why were they afraid after Jesus was crucified?

What must we do to prosper from His plan?

Key thought for today:

You're Not Listening!
John 3:5-8

What is required of us in order to enter God's kingdom?

How can you be born out of this world into His spirit?

Key thought for today:

The Cost of Oil!
Matthew 26:6-16

Why were they so upset with the woman who poured her oil on Jesus' feet?

Why did Jesus say it was harder for a rich man to go to Heaven than a camel to go through the eye of a needle?

Key thought for today:

Weaning From Tyranny!
1 Peter 4:1-2, 12-16

What do we need to do in order to be free from selfish dependencies?

What are some things in your life that need refining?

Key thought for today:

Reflection!
John 13:34-35

Is His light of love being reflected in your life today?

Should the stage of life that you are in affect your reflection of Him?

Key thought for today:

Let This Mind Be In You!
Philippians 2:5-11

How can we have the mind of Christ?

Are you willing to lay down yourself so that another may come to know Him? Willing to lay down your pride? Willing to be known as His? What does this look like for you?

Key thought for today:

The Divided!
Luke 19:38, 40

Are you so caught up in your daily life that you've allowed your relationship with God to become silent? If so, what are you doing to change it?

If today was The Day…what would you do? Who would you reach out to?

Key thought for today:

Lift Up Your Head!
Psalms 24:7-10

When your heart is hurting, Where do you turn? What is your source of relief?

Key thought for today:

Project And Reflect!
Psalms 4:5-8

Who or What are you reflecting in your life today?

Is it time for you to examine yourself and make a choice?
If so, what will it be?

Key thought for today:

Fruitful Bowels!

Galatians 5:22-26
(The Message and The King James version)

In these times of uncertainty and stress and the unknown, what kind of example are you?

Are you producing the fruits that draw people or are you just drawing fruit flies as you rot?

Key thought for today:

Would You Die For Me?
Romans 5:6-8

Would you give up your life for me? For anyone?

What are you doing with your life, that God sacrificed His own son for? How are you demonstrating God's love for you to others?

Key thought for today:

The Drive!
Joshua 1:8-9

What examples did God give Joshua to strengthen and encourage him?

What is driving you, where are you placing your hope?

Key thought for today:

In The Quiet!
Psalms 27:1, 4-5

How do you get refocused on Him when you are feeling overwhelmed? What/where is your quiet place?

Key thought for today:

Dry Bones!
Acts 4:23-26, 29-30

What do you desire to see God do in your life and those around you?

Key thought for today:

Friends!
Proverbs 27:9, 17-19

Do you have a special friend? Who and why are they special to you?

Key thought for today:

Weapons of Warfare!
Ephesians 6:10-12

When you are in the midst of a battle, what is your first reaction?

Do you have any "go to" verses that you keep in your arsenal?

Key thought for today:

Who Am I?
Psalms 68:1-4, 32-35

What do you think would happen if we spent more time celebrating who God is and talking about His greatness?

How do you see God?

Who is He to you today?

Key thought for today:

Masterpiece!
Proverbs 16:1-4, 7, 9

Have you ever had a "plan" go wrong and wondered why? Do you think God had another way that He wanted you to go and in the end it worked out better than you could've imagined?

What would you do differently now?

How does God want to make you His masterpiece?

Key thought for today:

Bottoms Up!
Proverbs 3:5-12

How can we live a Christian life when everything is so hard?

How do you tune in to His voice?

Key thought for today:

The Fog of Life!
1 Corinthians 13:12-13

How do you keep your focus on Him when difficult circumstances surround you?

Where do you find direction when your path is foggy?

Key thought for today:

The Report!
Habakkuk 3:17-19

Is there a circumstance that you have been praying about for some time? Have you been given a "bad report"?

What if He chooses to move in another way than you think He should? Will you listen to His voice?

Key thought for today:

Attention!
Matthew 6:34

Are you in need of a miracle? Are you pressing in and focusing on Him?

What is God's promise in Matthew 6:34?

Key thought for today:

Sum It Up!
1 Peter 3:8-12

What does this scripture say about giving and receiving blessings?

How can you turn a bad day into a good one?

Key thought for today:

Context Clues!
Jeremiah 29:10-14

What must we do in order to receive this promise from God?

How should we discipline ourselves to increase our knowledge and understanding of God's purpose in our life?

Key thought for today:

A Safe Place!
Psalms 46:1-3, 8-10

When you need a place of refuge from the storms of life do you immediately turn it over to God, or do you wrestle Him and try to control it yourself?

How do you feel when you finally let go and realize that God has your best interests at heart?

Key thought for today:

Get Your Glasses On!
James 1:25

Have you caught a glimpse of His promises but it keeps trying to slip away in the cares of the day? What does God say about this?

Key thought for today:

Sheer Gifts!
James 1:2-4, 12

Everyone faces challenges and tests, but not everyone has the skills to excel at these, where and how can you get help to hone these skills as needed?

What/Where is our battlefield?

Why is it considered a gift when we face battles?

Key thought for today:

In The Shadow!
Psalms 91:1-13

Why must we suffer if God's promises are true?

Time to shift your focus; Do your problems matter in eternity?

Will it change where you spend eternity?

Will it affect how someone else spends eternity?

Key thought for today:

Worship Is The Key!
Psalms 34:8-9, 17-18, 20

What are some ways you can get the best God has for you?

Key thought for today:

Search And Direct!
Psalms 139:1-3, 23-24

Are you trusting God with your heart?

Key thought for today:

Fire Me Up!
2 Samuel 7:18-24

Who are we to Him?

Are you seeking him?

Key thought for today:

Listen To Understand!
1 John 4:4-6

How do we tell the Spirit of Truth from the spirit of deception?

Key thought for today:

No Fretting Allowed?
Philippians 4:6-7

Does where you put your focus really matter?

Do you need to re-center today?

Key thought for today:

The Bargain!
Luke 11:10-13

Why does He fill some and not others in a "timely" manner?

Ask the Holy Spirit to fill you to overflowing today?

Key thought for today:

The Practice!
1 John 3:18-20

Why does He call us to be His hands extended?

Have you ever had an experience like this? How did it make you feel?

Whose reality will you see today?

Key thought for today:

The Woman of Great Value!
Proverbs 31:10-12, 25-26, 28, 30-31

What do you think is a woman of great value?

Key thought for today:

Protuberance!
1 John 5:4-5, 13-15

How do God's people stand out?

When we put on the mantle of His authority, what power do we achieve?

Key thought for today:

The Rock of Wait!
Psalms 40:1-3

What is the key to entering the mystery of all that is His?

Key thought for today:

The Tree!
Isaiah 55:8-11

If you are struggling today, cast His words over your life. Begin to speak His word as a statement of faith, that His promises will begin to take root. What promise are you holding on to today?

Key thought for today:

www.ingramcontent.com/pod-product-compliance
Lightning Source LLC
Chambersburg PA
CBHW041154120626
46547CB00020B/3207